CRIME SCENE DO NOT CROSS

POLICE LINE D

CRIME SCEN

POLICE LINE DO NOT CROSS

Officer Dan
Looks for
CLUES

An introduction to forensic
science for kids

Written by Daniel Anselment
Illustrated by Amy Anselment

ISBN 978-0-9884766-0-8

www.OfficerDanBooks.com

Printed in the U.S.A.

This edition first printing, November 2012

Graphic Design by Jill Weddall, *Moxie Create, LLC,* www.moxiecreate.com

For Olivia, Caden, and Isabella—
May you forever be inspired and continue to dream.

We love you very much!

—Dad and Mom

Hello kids my name is Officer Dan.

I am your neighborhood police officer.

Today I am going to speak to you about types of clues I look for at a crime scene.

When someone steals something,
the police are called to the crime scene.

For example, yesterday I was called to a store
that had been broken into.

Someone had pried open the store's safe!

This is called a burglary.

To look for clues at the burglary scene,
I use many different tools to help me.

Flashlight

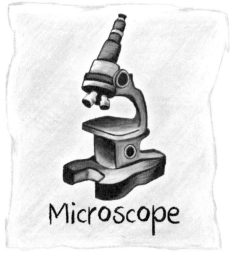

Microscope

Ruler

Tent Card

The tool I use the most is a digital camera.

I take pictures of the clues I find
with my camera.

This helps me to remember exactly what
the scene looked like,
which is very important.

Let's go over all the clues I found and
discuss how to collect each of them.

Our first clue is a fingerprint.

We are all born with fingerprints, but nobody has the same print as you.

Loop   Whorl   Arch

FACT: Our fingerprints are made up of loops, whorls, and arches.
Take a look at these examples;
What type of fingerprint do you have?

If you touch a table you will likely leave a fingerprint.

You may not be able to see your fingerprint, but I can use a special powder and brush to dust over the fingerprint to make it appear.

Once I find the fingerprint, I lift it off the table using a piece of clear tape.

Another clue I look for at a crime scene is a shoeprint. If you step in the dirt you will likely leave a shoeprint. Shoeprints can be found in different types of surfaces such as dirt, snow, or sand.

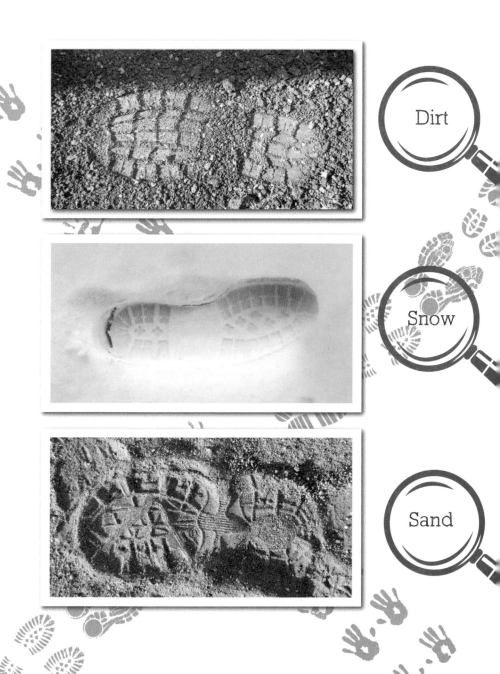

Dirt

Snow

Sand

In this case the burglar stepped in mud outside the door.

When the burglar stepped in the mud, his shoe sunk down leaving a nice shoeprint as you can see this in the photo.

I can use a shoeprint to show that someone was at the scene of the crime.

If I find someone walking in the same area as the burglary, I would check the bottom of their shoes to see if the shoeprint matches the print left in the mud.

Another clue I look for is tool marks.

Tool marks are often found on door or window frames.

A tool mark is left when someone uses a screwdriver or pry bar to force open a door or window.

In this case you can see the burglar pried open the side door on the business.

Tool marks can be made in different surfaces such as wood, metal or painted surfaces.

Let's look at one example of a tool marking as seen on this door frame.

Another clue I look for at the scene is hair that may have been left by someone.

Hair can be used to help identify the person who was at the crime scene.

FACT: It is thought that we lose 80-100 strands of hair each day.
Did you know you have about 80,000 to 100,000 hairs growing on your head?

Some of us have thick coarse hair and some of us have fine thin hair.

Some people even have curly hair.

Our hair can be cut to different lengths, and each of us has a different color to our hair.

QUESTION:

What color is your hair?

Do you have curly, straight, short or long hair?

Another clue I look for at a crime scene are fibers.

Fibers come from our clothing.

If you look closely at the carpet next to the where the safe was located, it looks like there may be a fiber which might belong to the burglar.

Microscope

Under a microscope I can match fibers found on a person and compare it to the fibers left at the scene.

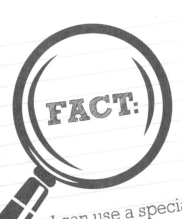

FACT:

I can use a special flashlight that makes fibers glow, making it easier for me to find.

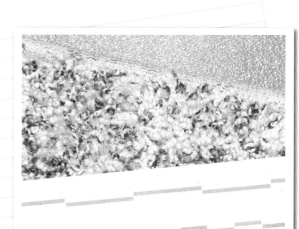

QUESTION:

Can you find a loose fiber on your shirt or pant leg? It is easier to find a light colored fiber if you are wearing dark colored clothing.

After I take pictures of the clues,
I collect each clue by packaging it up
to keep it safe at the police station.

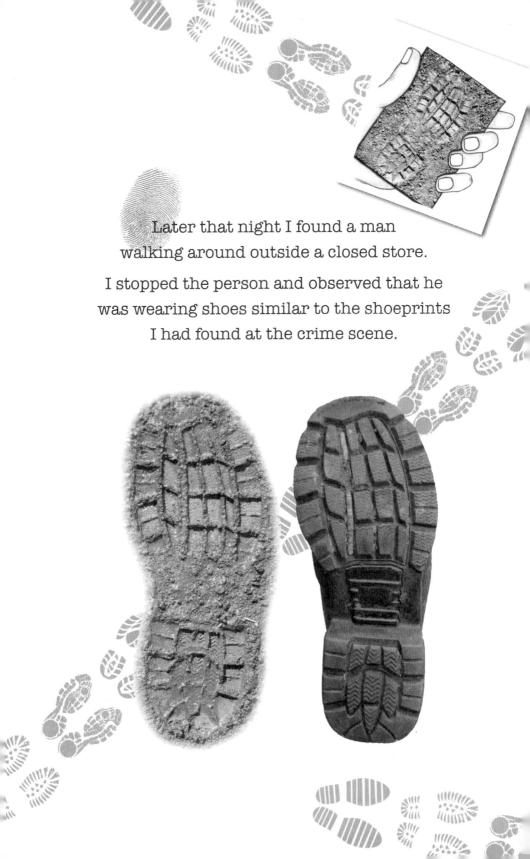

Later that night I found a man
walking around outside a closed store.

I stopped the person and observed that he
was wearing shoes similar to the shoeprints
I had found at the crime scene.

This person was also carrying tools similar to the markings I found on the door frame.

He was also wearing a shirt with the same fibers we found on the carpet in the store.

The burglar was caught!

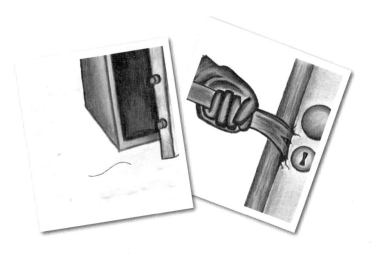

Everything we talked about today is a
part of forensic science.

I hope you learned something new and exciting.

Remember, not only am I a police officer
but I am also your friend.